HULL FAIR

An Illustrated History

by

Stephen Smith and Kevin Scrivens

HUTTON PRESS
1991

Published by The Hutton Press Ltd.
130 Canada Drive, Cherry Burton,
Beverley, East Yorkshire HU17 7SB

Copyright © 1991

No part of this book may be reproduced, stored in a
retrieval system, or transmitted in any form, or by any
means electronic, mechanical, photocopying, recording
or otherwise, without the prior permission of the
Publisher and the Copyright Holders.

Printed and bound by
Clifford Ward & Co. (Bridlington) Ltd.
55 West Street, Bridlington,
East Yorkshire YO15 3DZ

ISBN 1 872167 26 8

DEDICATION

This book is dedicated to Ron Smith for all his help.

ACKNOWLEDGEMENTS

The authors would like to thank the following people who have contributed in some way in the preparation of this book: Roger Alford; Roy Carlton; Mr. A. Cook; Graham Downie; Tommy Green; Chris Ketchell; John Ling; Bernard Mitchell; Mr. F. Sanderson; Michael Smith; Jack Schofield; Rowland Scott; Malcolm Slater; Mr. M. Thatcher; Mr. M. Willis (Aerofilms Ltd.).

We would also like to thank the staff at the Local History Section of Hull Central Library and Mr. Andrew Mellor and the staff at The World's Fair Ltd. in Oldham for their help during research.

INTRODUCTION

In 1888 the *Hull Critic* claimed that "a large number of people in Hull...look forward to the eleventh of October long before it arrives." It was, of course, referring to Hull Fair, which had just been found a new home on Walton street. The history of the fair goes back to the time when the town, then known as Wyke upon Hull, was the property of the Abbot of Meaux.

In 1278 the Abbot petitioned King Edward I for a Royal Charter. An inquisition was held in York that year, and Wyke was allowed a fair in one of 4,860 such charters granted during the Middle Ages. The first fair in the town took place between 9th and 23rd March, in the grounds of Holy Trinity.

For two weeks the churchyard was filled with traders, pedlars and merchants. It is not surprising that complaints were made as priests found it difficult to make themselves heard above the din caused by the fair. A new law, passed in 1282, made it illegal to hold such events in church grounds. Fairs were moved from graveyard to market place; thus Wyke's fair was resited.

As a port, many goods could be bought at the Fair which were not normally available: merchants brought wine from Gascony, corn, fish and whale oil from Norway, timber, pitch and furs from the Baltic, and, of course, the rich spices and silk from the Orient. In addition to the traders and merchants came itinerant entertainers: street players, acrobats and musicians. Performing animals became a common sight at English fairs, as well as more cruel sports.

The late 13th Century was a troubled time for Edward I. His two chief adversaries, France and Scotland, were to ensure that England had but brief periods of peace until the end of the Middle Ages. Amidst this turmoil King Edward acquired the town of Wyke upon Hull from the Abbot of Meaux.

As his property, Edward renamed the settlement Kingston upon Hull, and it became one of several new towns established at the time, including Leeds and Liverpool. An entry in the Calendar of Rolls, dated 1st July, 1293, tell us that the fair at Kingston upon Hull was to begin on the "Eve of St. Augustine the Archbishop, and lasting until the Eve of the Translation of St. Thomas the Martyr". For six weeks stalls and entertainers took over the Market Place, spreading into Lowgate and Whitefriargate.

In 1299 Edward granted a Royal Charter to the town, giving Hull the status of a free borough. It allowed the burgesses "one fair in every year, to continue for thirty days, namely on the day of St. Augustine after Easter [May 26th], and for twenty-nine days following, unless...that fair shall be to the injury of neighbouring markets and fairs".

During the Middle Ages the character of the fair would have altered little. Medieval towns cannot have been pleasant places to live, with the problems of public health. The annual fair can only have exacerbated the situation. Streets were narrow and already overcrowded. Hardly surprising that when an epidemic hit the country it had catastrophic effects. Following the Plague the fair dwindled.

In the later Middle Ages, the Burgesses were able to keep a tighter control over the fair when the custom of the "Pie Powder" courts was introduced. Actually a corruption of *pied poudre*, it offered an opportunity for arbitration in disputes arising at the fair.

Concerned by the "ungodly" and "wicked playes" which were performed during the fair, the Mayor and Alderman fined visitors to such booths 2s 6d for the offence. They were worried about the "divers idle and lewd persons, players or setters-out of plays and interludes who frequented the town". Such players or owners of the play-houses could be fined up to 20s. Bishop Poore also showed contempt for the "vile and indecorous games which tempt unseemliness".

During the reign of Queen Elizabeth I, a new Royal Charter, granted on 21st August, 1598, gave the Mayor and the Burgesses permission to hold an annual mart for fifteen days beginning on the 16th September "yearly and every year". By the seventeenth century fairs were becoming more carefree, with Wild Beast shows and satirical theatre.

Plague and war hit the seventeenth century. Following the epidemic in which over 700 of Hull's inhabitants died, a law was passed stating "that no more than eight people should assemble together". The fair was cancelled in 1637 in an attempt to prevent the disease spreading, and the following year no goods were allowed to unload in Hull for the fair.

When Hull successfully held out against the Royalists in 1643 the town celebrated, making 11th October a day of thanksgiving. This disappeared in the Restoration, but locking the town's gates against Charles I in the Civil War apparently left Charles II with no grudge against Hull. When the town's charter was surrendered, he immediately granted another on 3rd December 1661, confirming the privileges given by Elizabeth I. The fair now commenced on the 29th September; the change of date may have occurred as a result of the Plague or the Civil War.

In 1751 the country "lost" eleven days so that Britain's calendar should correspond with the facts of astronomy. When the day after September 2nd became the 14th, mobs went around the streets howling, "Give us back our eleven days," imagining their lives had somehow been shortened. This caused the day for Hull Fair to change and be advanced to 11th October.

CHAPTER ONE

With the Industrial Revolution came safer and faster transport, mass production and factories, making redundant the old trading fairs. It seemed that they were in imminent danger of dying out, as was the livelihood of the itinerant showmen who provided amusements at them. Thomas Frost, writing in 1874, claimed that "the last showman will soon be as great a curiosity as the dodo".

Whilst Hull was expanding as a major port, it made it difficult to find a suitable location for the fair. Building land for warehouses and new docks was needed, and each time new developments took place, a new site had to be found. Increasing volumes of traffic in the Market Place made it too congested to cope with the fair, so when Humber Dock was built, the fair moved into Humber Street, Nelson Street, Wellington Street and Queen Street.

William Bradley, the "Yorkshire Giant" was amongst the attractions at Hull Fair in 1815. The tallest Englishman ever recorded charged 1s for visitors to meet him in Queen Street during the fair. Bradley, born in Market Weighton, stood 7'9" high, and had been introduced to George III and members of the Royal Family at Windsor. Although the fair prospered in this location, it was only a temporary home.

Little Dock Green, approached by way of Castle Street, became the site for the 1836 Hull Fair. The land was used as a play-ground by the Trinity House Boys, but the fair soon expanded into Railway Street, Kingston Street and Commercial Road. Visitors could watch drama at Wild's Picture Gallery whilst dancing and drinking carried on all day in Alger's Dancing Saloon. This booth, which measured 110' by 55', was brought to Hull by steamship from London. Another attraction in Castle Street was Springthorpe's Waxworks. Automatic figures performed outside the show to help draw crowds.

Part of the site was lost when Railway Dock was built in the 1840's, but more land was found between Humber Dock and Miller's Shipyard. Close by were Thomas Cooke's Royal Arena and "Loop-the-Loop" centrifugal railway.

H. J. Corlyon, a well-known Hull journalist with the *Globe* explains that "the stalls used to run the whole length of Wellington Street down Queen Street and Market Place. The fair at that time was commonly regarded as a good one". This early witness tells us that "there were invariably a Richardsonian show or two, swings, roundabouts galore, and what was a never-failing source of attraction and pleasure — Wombwell's Menagerie". Plays were often performed on a temporary stage erected outside the Apollo Rooms at the corner of Wellington Street.

Child labour was used to keep the fair going, especially for pushing the roundabouts round. Corlyon introduces us to Johnson, a tough, foul-mouthed showman who whipped his young workers rather more frequently than he rewarded them. Johnson and his wife, who presented their High Flying Swings, are singled out as a unique pair, being "universal favourites, notwithstanding their addiction to vituperation and unsavoury expletives". What surprised him was that despite the apparent cruelty towards his juvenile workers, Johnson was never short of volunteer labourers.

Land soon became so scarce that the fair was eventually moved out of the town. Its next home was Brown Cow Field on Anlaby Road. Now outside the town, many hoped the fair would die a natural death.

The 1853 fair is well documented by the *Hull Advertiser*. Amongst the stalls and shows which extended from Walker street to Luke Street, their reporter noted intinerant auctioneers, fat pigs and a young lady in spangles, a short petticoat and "a pair of most equivocal legs". There were, it reported further, "the roundabouts and swings in abundance".

Also amongst the attractions was Wombwell's Menagerie. One of the biggest shows on the road and, as one visitor claimed, one which "almost vies with the British Museum in its powers of bewildering the visitor by the wealth of its treasures". Another show was Calver's Marionettes, one of many popular puppet shows of the mid-nineteenth century fairground.

In 1861 the fair was again moved, the site chosen this time was near the old asylum at the end of Argyle Street. This instability resulted in petititions being made to the Corporation, and these, no doubt, encouraged the decision in 1865 to make available the Corporation Field in Park Street. Having lost its economic importance, the local authorities considered the fair to be a nuisance, and one which, given the opportunity, they would abolish.

Since Park Street was, for the greater part, occupied by respectable residences, its move was not a popular one locally. Corporation Field, opposite the Hull and East Riding College, was used for the Early Market every Tuesday and Friday morning, but complaints were soon made about the fair being held there. One witness claimed it was "a disgrace to the town" and described the ground as "a veritable quagmire".

Stalls were ranged on both sides of Park Street and Londesborough Street, and oyster and mussel stalls assembled along Spring Street, at the entrance to which was an American Photographic Studio. As *The Graphic* reported in 1882, the area became "especially lively once a year when it is the centre of the great Hull October Fair".

Park Street's residents must have been given renewed hope in their fight against the fair in 1871 when the Government claimed that "certain of the fairs in England are unnecessary, are the cause of grievous immorality, and are very injurious to the inhabitants of the towns in which such fairs are held". This indictment in the Fairs Act went so far as to suggest that, "it is expedient to make provision to facilitate the abolition of such fairs".

Roundabouts with horses, bicycles and boats for visitors to ride on appeared at the fair in 1882, along with the increasingly popular shooting galleries and swing boats. One showlady cracked her whip over the shins of the boys recruited to push her ride round if she thought they were shirking.

Just as steam made an important contribution to the Industrial Revolution, so it brought about a revolution on the fairgrounds. Traction engines, known as Showman's Road Locomotives allowed showmen to travel larger and heavier equipment, and they could generate for electric lights. Steam engines could also power roundabouts and so a new generation of rides appeared: the Galloping Horses, Switchbacks and Steam Yachts.

Steam was also used to power the "Military Band" organs which were often used to attract crowds to the shows. Another visitor to Hull Fair describes these: "We reached a rather pretentious booth. At the entrance was a wooden case containing a miniature brass band, played of course by steam. We next passed a yellow bedecked chariot with huge letters on the side proclaiming it to be the abode of the 'Amazonian Giantess' some seven feet six inches in length".

Each October hundreds of temporary stalls and bazaars were erected tempting children to buy toys and sweets. Saloons sent forth the aroma of boiling peas. Waxworks displayed the statues of the famous and infamous and Aunt Sally stalls rewarded the successful with cigars. Parts of the city were, as Tom Sheppard has described, "transformed into a very Bedlam with roundabouts, swings, shooting galleries, travelling menageries, circuses, sea serpents, double-headed oxen, jugglers, in fact anything likely to cause circulation of the coin in the well-filled pockets of the country visitors".

Amongst the attractions at Hull Fair in the 1880s was again Wombwell's Menagerie, with eight Lions, the Royal Bengal Tigers, Bears, Wolves. Hyenas, Leopards and Elephants. To view this collection cost 1s, or 6d for children. Days also presented their Menagerie with Wallace, the Famous Giant Lion, Captain Omgoso, "the most daring lion hunter in the world" and a lady snake charmer. Clark's Ghost Show visited the fair, performing the ghost illusion achieved by the use of a sheet of plate glass positioned at 45 degrees to the stage.

The *Hull Critic* visited the fair in 1885 during inclement weather. The behaviour of those attending the fair was considered better than usual, although the rain and efforts of the clerk "have had a salutory influence". The reporter gives us a further glimpse of the attractions of the fair. "There has been," he tells us, "the usual disgusting amount of fat females exhibited and the customary peep show with its pictures bordering so close to obscenity that it is remarkable the extremely good...authorities in Hull have not had a word to say on the matter".

Further problems from the move to Park Street soon became apparent. Pick-pockets congregated amongst the large crowds visiting the fair. Neither did it help that the site was not owned wholly by the Corporation, who lost revenue to Mr. Alderson who owned the remainder of the land used. It brought into question the Corporation's ability to provide a suitable location, and its commitment to the fair.

Although the fair prospered on the site, as did local traders who placed special advertisements in local newspapers, the residents never accepted it. According to the *Critic*, each year they "have been annoyed to boiling point of rage and the quantity of catarrah caused by the sloppy condition of the fairground is unlimited". Without too long a delay, Hull Corporation were again looking for an alternative location.

CHAPTER TWO

In April, 1888, Hull Corporation chose a new site in Beeton's Ville, off Anlaby Road. Mr. James Beeton had bought the land in the 1850s, and the streets were named after his daughters, sisters and nieces. The most easterly of these, adjoining the North Eastern Railway, was Walton Street. The Horse Fair was already being held there by 1887. Six acres of land between the street and the railway line were adopted by the Corporation for the fair.

To many, when Hull Fair was "relegated to the dismal wilds of Newington", it was an astute move and they hoped it would "soon be starved to death". There were those, however, who felt that the fair was "an old time institution which it would be little less than sacrilege to destroy". The *Hull Critic* pointed out that Park Street was not a fit place for the "noisy revelry" of the fair, but it did give happiness to "hundreds of poor children in whose lives, God knows, there is little enough of merry making".

Many showmen and councillors considered that the move was tantamount to abolishing the fair. Little was reported of the 1888 event; most local newspapers were preoccupied by the Whitechapel Murders. That year's fair must have given the anti-fair lobby even more hope. Although £550 had been spent on transforming the wasteland into a fairground, the new location was not popular with the travellers who attended: Thomas Chilman, the Corporation Market Keeper, reported that "the smaller stalls did very badly". The festivities included the horse and cattle fair as well as the entertainment, but some fair stalls were still reported as using the traditional Market Place in the town centre.

Chilman reported that he had been "exposed to a great deal of abuse by those who have been unsuccessful, and have had a great deal of trouble getting money from those persons". Charges ranged from 4d per foot for gingerbread stalls to £4 for a roundabout. The revenue from the event fell to £224 15s 6d, nearly £60 less than the income from the previous year's fair.

Amongst the attractions at early Hull Fairs were Waddington's Alpine Mountain Switchback, claimed to be "the only one lit up by The Electric Light" and Green's Patented Steeplechase Switchback Gallopers: "You've heard of the cow jumping over the moon", the *Critic* tells us, "the feat isn't in it with the jolly leaps Green's quadrupeds give you". Aspinall's Switchback was another attraction at the fair with its "stationary umbrella top" which was described by one contemporary source as "a fine and wonderful new innovation".

Amongst the showmen present was Randall Williams, the proprietor of "The Greatest Ghost Show in the World". This seated 1000, and as well as all the interior scenery, Williams brought his own traction engine for the purpose of lighting the show by electricity.

Great excitement was caused by 1896 when Randall Williams gave the people of Hull their first sight of moving pictures. His Bioscope Show caused a sensation, making the first appearance at any fair in the country, only months after the first public showing of films at the Polytechnic in London. Views of "Rush Hour on London Bridge" and "London's Fire Brigade" were amongst the first films exhibited.

Attractions in 1896 also included Pedley's Fine Art Show, a rather grandiose title for a peep show exhibiting risque tableaux. Pat Collins brought his Pneumatic Bicycle Roundabout, "the safest and healthiest sport for old and young, ladies and gentlemen". He also presented his "Venetian Gala Gondolas, the only real Gondolas at the fair, fitted with rolling motion". Pat Collins further pointed out that his was the "most elaborately decorated and costliest machine in existence".

Music for his rides was "produced by electricity on the latest musical instrument, the Gavioliphone". Collins explains that this was "not a noisy brass or barrel organ, but a scientific instrument, equivalent to a string band of 60 performers".

Terraces, public houses and a church had been built along the western side of Walton street by 1897, and for the first time the street itself was filled with even more stalls, shows and attractions. By now the fair was becoming well established at its new location, and extra excursion trains, ferries and wagonettes were laid on to bring the huge crowds who flocked to it.

In 1897, as well as being able to see a film of the Queen's Diamond Jubilee procession at Randall Williams' Bioscope Show, visitors could enjoy Councillor George Thomas Tuby's Galloping Horses and Steam Switchback, Lieske's Gigantic Wheel, Burke's Steam Swings, and William Marshall's Bicycles. In addition were no less than five other sets of steam horses.

The City of Hull Tramways opened the Anlaby Road extension in 1899. Now a visitor could take a tram along Anlaby Road, alight at Walton Street, traverse through the multitudes of stalls and onto the fairground. Here they might have taken a ride on Aspland's, Marshall's, Murphy's or Waddington's Switchbacks, Green's Racing Bantams, or even Pat Collins' Giant Cockerels. They could also have visited the circuses of Proctors and Baileys, watched Cottrell's Swimming Show or seen moving pictures at the Cinematograph Shows presented by Randall Williams, Enoch Farrar and George Aspland.

By 1906 the *World's Fair* was already describing the event as "England's largest fair". Thousands of visitors crowded into Walton Street each day. Train loads of visitors were brought into the town by the various railway companies, and the City Tramways did tremendous business. Mr. Grace was the Market Superintendent in 1906 and his layout has survived the ground's gradual expansion.

Nearly twenty roundabouts attended the 1906 Fair. Near to Walton Street were Relph and Pedley's Razzle Dazzle, Morley's Swings and William Murphy's Motor Switchback. Opposite these was another row of roundabouts, including Pat Collins' Motor Switchback, on which "drivers were requested not to exceed the speed limit". John Collins, who presented his Galloping Horses, also brought his Steam Yachts *Emperor* and *Empress*. "A sail in them," Collins claimed, "will do you the world of good". "They appealed," he went on to say, to "young and old fishermen, sailors and especially the ladies". Nearby was Lieske's Revolving Cars, an early steam-driven big wheel.

In another row heading back towards Walton Street was Pat Collins' Giant Racing Cockerels. Mr. J. W. Waddington announced that "the original inventor of the Motor Car roundabout has arrived with his Racing Motor Cars". Other rides included George Green's Racing Bantams with its distinctive Pagoda top, Aspland's Motor Switchback, Goldthorpe Marshall's Motor Switchback, Shipley's Galloping Horses, and William Henry Marshall's Flying Motors. Also present at the 1906 fair were Aspland & Howden's Flying Airship and Holdsworth's Slip, the first Helter Skelter to appear at Hull.

Each October the trams were taxed to their utmost capacity. The Corporation admitted that one tram took more money in one day during the fair, than a single car normally took in a fortnight. Electricity was also making the fair an attraction in another way. Showmen were quick to realise the potential of electric lights, and the fair became quite a spectacle at night; in 1908 the *World's Fair* described the carnival as "Light City".

For the 1908 fair, the Corporation had made available a larger than usual site, doubling the amount of land used from six to twelve acres. This made it the largest fairground in England. According to the *World's Fair*, the showmen's newspaper, "Hull Fair has again had a record number of attractions, and the splendid weather has been the means of larger crowds than ever visiting this famous carnival". The attractions included no less than seven of the finest Cinematograph concerns on the road. A new novely that year was a ride called the Cake Walk.

George Green advertised his first visit to Hull with his Argyle model tonneau de-luxe Motor Cars, "the most luxurious cars at the fair". Randall Williams advertised in the *Hull Daily Mail* that he was presenting the "largest and most powerful organ in the world" on the front of his Bioscope Show. The ground was packed with Shooting Saloons, Emma stalls and ring boards, while along Walton Street there were rows of bazzars, numerous gingerbread stalls, hundreds of tale tellers, hand sellers, quid givers, etc. "without doubt making the biggest fair held in England".

Threatened by attacks from Members of Parliament and Councillors, the travelling showmen had formed a trade association in 1889 to protect their business. Whilst the fair was closed on Sunday, the Showmen's Guild held their annual meeting. Hull's Mayor was asked to take the chair, and speakers included the Rev. T. Horne, the Guild's Honorary Chaplain. The gathering took place in one of the shows, such as Farrar and Tyler's Cinematograph Show, which hosted the group in 1908.

Perhaps concerned by the public's attitudes to the showmen's itinerant lifestyle, the Mayoress of Hull was invited into several of the living vans belonging to the show proprietors. Here she saw how elaborately furnished they were: in one an apartment was fitted up like a dainty little drawing room, and on the table, which slid in and out, was an artistic tea service. The fireplace was polished like silver, and Royal Worcester adorned the mantlepiece. The main difficulty encountered by the ladies was that the ample hats then in fashion were wider than the narrow doorways to the caravans.

On Sunday the various Christian churches occupied the front of the shows for services or meetings. Socialist speakers were amongst the preachers, and concerts in aid of the charities were given on the front of Bostock and Wombwell's Menagerie.

Twenty-seven railway excursions brought over 12,000 people into Newington Station on 10th october, 1908. Crowds poured down Walton Street and the fairground was thickly crowded, bringing brisk business for the showmen. The Hull and Barnsley Railway Company and the Great Central also contributed their quota, giving a dense but orderly crowd by the evening. So busy were the rides that they had to increase their prices to cope with the numbers.

Messrs. Farrar and Tyler made an important breakthrough in 1910 when they brought the first Electric Scenic Railway to Hull. They claimed it was "the finest invention in electrical science as applied to amusements ever introduced to a discriminating public". A local journalist reported that "this railway must not be confounded with the old fashioned steam driven switchbacks", and the owners claimed further that "real motor cars...travelling at 60 m.p.h." gave riders a journey, "over mountains and valleys through beautiful Alpine scenery".

Teddy Bears were one great craze in 1910, and Pat Collins' "Racing Teddy Bears" attended the fair that year. The Joy Wheel was another. Green's brought their "House that Jack Built", a building said to be of "the early English style, although one visitor added that "a great surprise lay in store for all who enter therein".

Chipperfield's Menagerie featured the "Elephant Boy" in 1912 which proved a great attraction. Side shows were less inhibited by public taste in the past. Amongst the other human attractions were Harold Pyott, the smallest man and Frederick the Great, a 19 year old lad standing 8' tall and weighing 22 stone. Tom Wortley presented the three-legged girl and Christina the Tattooed Princess and Brose Harvey secured a fine novelty with Dyena, the Serpent Dancer. Another show featured "The Convict City", a working model made by the inmate of an asylum during his fifteen year sentence.

Objections were raised in 1914 by Hull Chamber of Commerce, who considered that it would be "undesirable to hold a fair during the present crisis". Their concern that 'airships would be attracted by the brilliant lights," was ignored in 1914, and Hull Fair went ahead, but it was cancelled the following year. When the official Peace Souvenir was printed in Hull in 1919 it was "believed that Hull Fair will be revived with unabated vigour".

CHAPTER THREE

1919 saw the return of Hull Fair to Walton Street. Missing in post war years were the Cinematograph Shows. Projection equipment became too bulky and films too expensive. By 1918 Hull had over 20 permanent cinemas, including the nearby West Park Picture Palace. Mander's Famous Waxworks was another victim of changing tastes; at the 1919 fair, it was presented as a Menagerie.

The passing of the old allowed space for new developments. Over twenty rides appeared at the 1920 fair, including five Electric Scenic Railways, three Steam Switchbacks, four sets of Galloping Horses, three sets of Steam Yachts and six Cake Walks.

By 10 o'clock on October 11th "a dozen or two steam organs had struck up playing the latest ragtime tunes and music hall numbers, selections from the operas and items of classical music". Bostock and Wombwell's Menagerie had arrived in Hull by special train from Nottingham Goose Fair. According to the *Hull Daily Mail* the fair was back to "its pre-war glory".

Many showmen used the railways to move their waggons, and they were unloaded and brought to the fairground behind the showmen's engines. One contemporary report describes the "great steam engines with tall smoke stacks and huge wheels which grind their way over the roads of Hull that lead to Walton Street, trailing behind them swaying waggons stacked high with gigantic painted horses and all the rest of the showmen's stock-in-trade".

One ride which came to Hull by rail was Reuben Holdsworth's "Racing Porkers". This favourite ride was distinctive as it rotated anti-clockwise, although the top spun the opposite way. As well as the racing Pigs, the ride also featured two "Waltzing Balloons".

After being unloaded at the station, the waggons were hauled to Walton Street behind the powerful and ornate showmen's engines. Sometimes these caused so much vibration that the residents of Spring Bank West were forced to complain about the "violent trembling and cracking of walls" which they suffered.

Confetti was still being sold at Hull Fair in 1921, making it one of the last fairs in the north to continue the tradition. As well as getting into girls' clothes, the showmen complained that it got into the engines' lubricating oil and organ pipes. So even at Hull the tradition passed. Showmen were always eager to have their fair-organs playing the latest tunes: the hit for 1921 was "Swanee".

In an attempt to improve the site, in 1922 the Corporation rolled clinker into the ground. However, only two years later, the *Hull Daily Mail* reported the "shocking state of Hull Fair Ground", which, they claimed was still "like a quagmire of liquid mud", They reported how the "showmen were working feverishly, unloading freshly-arrived lorries, putting the finishing touches to wonderful contraptions in the shape of scenic railways and attempting, almost futilely, to remove mud from everything".

At exactly twelve noon, Hull Fair 1924 swung into action. The first fair-organ to strike up played "Pasadena" and all the rides opened for business. Crowds of "mud-splashed though happy children" cared more about catching the low afternoon prices than the state of their clothes. The latest novely was "Over the Falls", brought by Pat Collins M.P. On the Sunday evening Goldthorpe Marshall gave a sacred concert on the organ in his Proud Peacock scenic Railway. The proceeds were for the St. John's Ambulance Brigade.

On Monday 12th October 1925, Hull Fair received its first official civic opening. It was performed by Alderman C. Raine, and took place on the front of Bostock and Wombwell's "Royal No.1 Menagerie", which claimed was making its 120th annual visit to the city's fair.

In 1925 the reporter for the *World's Fair* noticed that many of the gardens, passages and bits of land in Walton Street were all occupied, "from the humble toy seller to the more aristocratic palmist with her saloon motor landaulette". Amongst the games which now opened at Hull Fair were Spinners, Discs, the Spider, Climbing Monkeys, Coconut sheets, Darts and Roll-ups.

Fire was always a concern for both the showmen and the Corporation. In 1928 £1,000 worth of damage was done to toy stalls when a Naphtha Flare Lamp hanging on one of the stalls fell. These lamps were subsequently banned from the ground, but by the 1920s most showmen were using carbon Arc Lamps which gave brighter light.

At the opening ceremony of the 1931 fair, the Mayor, Alderman Farmery, broke the sad news that this was positively the last visit to Hull Fair of Bostock and Wombwell's Travelling Zoo. The Mayor commended the show from both an educational and entertaininng standpoint, and announced that the animals were going to Whipsnade. Since the show had been coming to Hull since 1805 it was certainly no stranger to the city.

It is a tribute to the show's manager, Harold Birkett, that the Menagerie opened at Selby for a night between Nottingham Goose Fair, which closed on 3rd October, and Hull Fair, which opened on October 12th.

1931 was the last year that Market Superintendent William Salmon was in charge of the fair. He had served since 1925, and had always ensured that the organisation ran smoothly. Alderman Farmery explained in his opening address how the fair left Hull Corporation with "a handsome rent after providing the citizens with a week's enjoyment". This totalled £2,955 in 1931.

Another change for 1931 was noted by the *World's Fair* with not one Electric Scenic Railway present. The new Novelty Rides had taken their place. Their debut was marked by the appearance of Pat Collins' Swish in 1926, and the 1930s witnessed a revolution in fairground attractions. As usual hundreds of stalls stretched for almost three-quarters of a mile along Walton Street, while the fairground itself housed two circuses, five Dodgems, five Noah's Arks, two Swirls, four sets of Steam Roundabouts, a Monkey Speedway, 100 hooplas and other stalls.

Scenic Railways were heavy and cumbersome to move, requiring up to nine waggons. They also proved too slow for the modern generation, who wanted Speed and Thrills. So the Scenics and Switchbacks gave way to the Speedways and Dodgems.

The passing of Bostock and Wombwell's Menagerie also marked a change in the side shows: Pat Collins presented a Wall of Death with Fearless Egbert, who drove a minature car with "Monarch" a lion, as passenger. This is said to have taken Hull by storm, as queues of people eagerly awaited this spectacular show. Other novelties appearing at Hull that year were Pat Collins' "Death in the Guillotine Show", and Charles Thurston's "Monkey Speedway".

Tippler White brought side shows to Hull Fair for many years. In 1931 he had to assure the people of Hull that Mary Ann Bevans, the "Ugliest Woman an Earth" was not dead, but would be appearing at the fair, along with La Belle Eve, claimed to be France's most perfect woman. Bert Hughes was another familiar character with his famous Boxing Pavilion. Before a performance he would bring a youth onto the front of the show and slice a raw potato in half on the boy's palm, with his sword, without leaving so much as a scratch. He would then offer cash prizes for any local fighters who could stand the pace against one of his lads.

Causing something of a sensation at the fair in 1931 was the Palm Beach Amusement Company's gigantic Figure-8 Railway, which built up on a new ground utilising the allotments previously along the front of Walton Street. Fourteen acres of ground were now occupied by the fair.

The following year saw even more new novelties. Collins presented his Nap Hand: "the greatest attractions ever staged in Hull". This included the only Water Dodgem ever operated at a travelling fair, requiring no less than 50,000 gallons of water to fill it. His other attractions included the original Mont Blanc, the only Yo-Yo ride, which they claimed was "the rage of Nottingham Goose Fair", an Indian Theatre, a Ghost Train and the Wall of Death.

Amongst the other rides advertised were Green's Caterpillars and Jack Whyatt's Miss England Speedboats and The Swirl. Farrar's Mont Blanc offered "all the excitement of mountaineering from an armchair without any of the dangers" and Marshall's Hey Day, it was claimed, "will shake you up nicely and make you feel ready to fight Carnera".

Ling's presented their Ghost Train and Steam Yachts, but their most popular attraction was the grocery stall run by Joe Barak, alias "Chickn Joe". The prizes of groceries and chickens must have been welcome in many Hull households in the depression, so not surprisingly the stall was well patronised, being billed "Chicken Joe — The Man You All Know".

To generate the necessary power for all the rides, shows and lights needed dozens of showmen's engines, working long hours. Each time an engine was stoked, clouds of dense black smoke were emitted. To try to make the fairground brighter, and more hygienic Hull Corporation Electricity Committee began to supply power to the showmen in 1932. Many showmen began to take advantage of the supplies around the ground, more especially the stall-holders. The Corporation tried to attract showmen by explaining that it was a great deal less wear and tear on their engines, and tons of coal would be saved. Nor would they have to pull water barrels through the crowds whilst the fair was open.

As early as 1933 the showmen were trying to persuade the Corporation to allow the fair to run over two weekends. It was supposed to be in deference to local shopkeepers that the fair was restricted to just a single week. A deputation from the Showmen's Guild met with the Markets and Abattoirs Committee, but no extension was granted. They claimed it would incur an additional expense of about £220. The receipts from that year's fair were a record £3,456!

In 1933 Enoch Clifford Farrar presented the first Waltzer at the Fair. This had been new only weeks earlier at Woodhouse Feast in Leeds. Another new novelty in 1938 was Joe Ling's futuristic Moonrocket. When, however, World War Two broke out in September 1939, Walton Street Fairground was requisitioned for military purposes, and the fair was again disrupted during the years of hostilities.

CHAPTER FOUR

In 1945 concern began to mount as to whether Hull Fair would be held that year. Walton Street fairground was still requisitioned for military purposes, but the authorities released it temporarily until October 21st to allow the fair to go ahead. The Mayor, Alderman Wheelhouse, said that if any place in the country was entitled to relaxation it was the battered city of Hull.

Although the 1945 Fair was not quite up to pre-war standards it must have been welcomed by many. The war was still very much on people's minds, and the showmen realised this. Joe Ling's Steam Yachts were presented as the "Victory Swings" and the boats were re-named "Monty" and "Winnie" in honour of the wartime heroes. Other attractions included Lace's Victory Roll and Walker's Rollicking Jeep.

Soon Hull Fair had regained its reputation of being one of England's biggest. In 1947 the opening ceremony was performed on the front of Fossett's Circus. Amongst the rides was John Farrar's new "Odeon" style Waltzer, with huge art deco front.

In 1948 Pat Collins brought his famous Scenic Dragons out of retirement from Sutton Coldfield. It was almost twenty years since the last Scenic Railway opened at Hull, so the appearance of the Dragons and Peacocks, with the Marenghi organ and Burrell showman's engine "The Griffin" must have stirred fond memories. This solitary visit became something of a legend although the ride was scrapped at Sutton Coldfield in the early 1960s.

Hull was one of the few fairs where side shows continued in popularity. In post-war years Tom Norman's Palladium was one of the largest shows still travelling. A grand Marenghi organ, which had once stood in the centre of Harniess Brothers' Scenic Motors, attracted crowds to see the many and varied acts which Tom Norman presented. These included Tommy Jacobsen, the armless pianist, and Lieut. Comm. Ian Frazer V.C. and his team of frogmen.

Attitudes have altered towards the shows which exhibited people like the "Gorgeous and Glamorous Anita", the smallest woman on earth, just 22" high and weighing 75lb, and Titana, the Staffordshire Giantess who stood 6'2" and weighed over 35st. George the Gentle Giant is one of the few human attractions to appear in recent years.

Since the war the fair has continued to change and expand. In 1952 an additional Saturday was added, and in 1985 the opening was brought forward to the Friday evening. The problem of parking was eased when the Carriage Sheds were demolished, although the Corporation moved the vehicles off the central reservation on Spring Bank West.

Hull as a city has also expanded and more housing development on its eastern side called for a more central location for the fair. The danger looked even more apparent when the housing department condemned the terraces on Walton street, ripped them down and replaced them with council-owned properties.

Not all the new council-house tenants were so keen to share their street with the showmen and objected to the annual inconvenience. The old Walton Street residents had been brought up with the fair on their doorstep, and often rented out their front gardens to the showmen. It seemed inevitable that the Council would use the fourteen acre fairground opposite to build more houses.

"Keep Hull Fair on Walton Street" was the slogan which the Showmen's Guild adopted in their effort to avoid yet another move. The shortage of building land in Hull led to councillors considering using the fairground for building as many as 200 new homes. "It could be a very emotional matter", suggested Councilllor John Black, and indeed it was. Colin Noble, the President of the Showmen's Guild said: "We want to continue coming to Hull Fair on Walton street". The promise was made that even if the site was used the fair would continue, but finding an alternative site posed an even greater problem.

The docklands seemed to be favourite for a while, and councillors compared the move to 1927 when Nottingham Goose Fair was moved out to the Forest. The showmen remained unconvinced. Relief was felt when the centenary year saw the fair still on Walton Street, but still rumours abound of change and alternative sites are mentioned as regularly as the fair attends the city. Whether the fair will return to the old town where it began 700 years ago remains a matter of speculation.

Ironically in its centenary year the fair was again threatened, not by the Council, but this time by the ambitions of one showman who submitted plans to transform Walton Street into an American-style Theme Park. The plan met with overwhelming rejection, possibly because of the sheer naïvety and impracticality of the proposal, but possibly out of loyalty to the generations of travelling showmen who have attended Hull Fair for so many years.

Since the search for new ideas is an integral part of the showmen's business, each year brings new attractions. Even the

Waltzer and Dodgems are now becoming dated alongside the Matterhorn, Flying Carpet and Break Dance. It is now the descendants of the showmen who brought amusements to the fair in the last century who attend the Hull Fair. Names like Marshalls, Waddington, Green, Lings and Farrars represent well-founded travelling families.

The debate as to which is Britain's largest fair continues, but after over seven centuries, Hull Fair continues to thrive as one of the country's most important fairs.

SELECT BIBLIOGRAPHY

Books

BRAITHWAITE, David	Fairground Architecture Hugh Evelyn, London, 1968.
BRAITHWAITE, David	Savages of Kings Lynn Patrick Steves, Cambridge, 1975.
CORRIGAN, Edwin	Ups and Downs and Roundabouts Ridings Publishing Co. Driffield, 1972.
FRIED, Frederick	A Pictorial History of the Carousel Barnes and Co. New York, 1964.
MIDDLEMISS, John	A Zoo on Wheels Dalebrook Publications, Burton, 1987.
STARSMORE, Ian	English Fairs Thames and Hudson, London, 1975.
WALVIN, James	Leisure and Society Longman, London, 1978.
WEEDON, Geoff	Fairground Art White Mouse, London, 1981.

Newspapers and Periodicals:

The Hull Critic.
The Globe.
The Hull Daily Mail.
The World's Fair.
Fairground Mercury (Fairground Association of Great Britain).
Keyframe (Fair Organ Preservation Society).

Collections:

Thursford Steam Museum, Thursford, Norfolk.
The collection of steam engines and fair-organs includes Aspland's Gondola Switchback.

Wookey Hole Caves and Mill, Wookey Hole, Wells, Somerset.
The Lady Bangor Fairground Collection of art and carved-work.

THE EARLY YEARS 1888-1914

Waxworks Exhibitions had been popular at Hull for many years. Mander's show, seen here in 1904, was keeping apace of modern developments by also showing moving pictures. To the right of the show can be seen the portable steam engine used to generate for the electric arc lamps on the show-front.

A popular attraction when Hull Fair was held on Corporation Field was Clark's Ghost Show. This photograph was taken in the late nineteenth century. (M. Thatcher).

A rear shot of Lieske's Wheel, showing the upright boiler for the steam engine which powered the ride. (F. Sanderson).

One of the first Big Wheels to travel and a regular feature at Hull was M. Lieske's "Revolving Balloon Ride". Like many rides, a trumpet barrel organ stood at the front of the ride to attract riders. (T. Green).

Travelling at the turn of the century, when the roads were often little more than dirt tracks, cannot have been easy. William Murphy, whose Switchback regularly attended Hull Fair, used this Fowler showman's engine, named "Powerful", to pull the waggons onto which the roundabout packed. This 1895 view shows how many trucks a single engine could pull.

Amongst the attractions at Hull in 1896 was Pat Collins' Venetian Gala Gondolas, claimed to be the costliest machine at the fair. The lavish carved work can be seen in this early view of the ride.

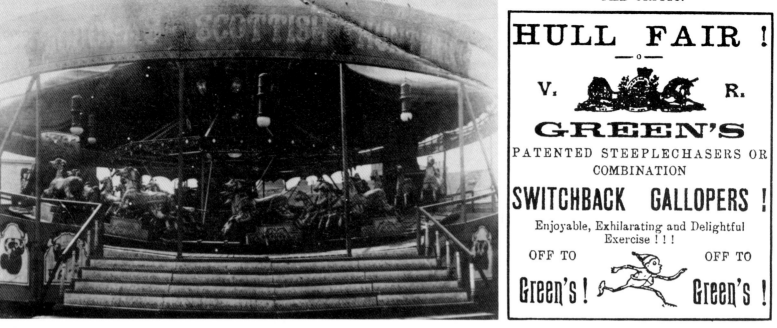

In 1890 George Green presented his "Patented Steeplechasers or Combination Switchback Gallopers" at Hull. This view shows the ride after it had been sold to another Scottish showman.

George Green brought a number of rides from Glasgow to Hull. This ride was known as his Racing Bantams. The pagoda style top, which was unique, was carved by Orton, Sons and Spooner. The roundabout was sold to America but the ship sank in the North Sea, and it had to be salvaged before opening on Coney Island.

This peep show went under the rather grandiose title of "Fine Art Gallery". This view of Enoch Farrar's show is a good example with elaborate carved work covering the front, as well as the mechanical organ in the centre between the entrances.

A trumpet barrel organ can be seen more clearly in this early shot of Chipperfield's Menagerie. Visiting shows of this kind gave many their only opportunity to see wild animals. The sign on the left reads: "This is a Menagerie, not a living picture show". (T. Green).

Looking down a row of roundabouts at the 1904 Fair. In the foreground is Green's Racing Bantams and to its left are the Switchbacks of Asplands and Marshalls.

Hull Fair, 1904, with Aspland's Switchback in the foreground. The Gondola cars were designed in 1894 and carved by Savages of King's Lynn. They feature square cupolas, whose ceilings are decorated with birds and clouds. Each car also has a carved royal head on the rear canopy. The notice on the front is warning the young lads watching that "All persons are requested to keep their feet off the seats". Mr. Aspland was obviously proud of his roundabout.

"Awarded the Gold Medal for Steadiness and No Flickering". This was the boast made by Captain Tom Payne in 1906. On the left of the show can be seen the fair-organ, while to the right is "The Sun", Payne's brand-new Fowler showman's engine.

A close up of the dancing girls on Payne's Show. Competition between the Bioscope Shows was becoming fierce by 1906. (T. Green).

Being itinerant forced most showmen to live in caravans or living waggons as they are more usually known. Here George Aspland, who attended Hull Fair from the 1860s, is seen outside his "House on Wheels". Notice how even the living waggons carried carved work, and how much their design was influenced by railway carriages.
(Fairground Heritage Trust).

An early view looking down Walton Street with the Drill Hall to the left. The tall wooden structure is the tower of the old original Long Switchback Railway. It is unlikely that this travelled and was probably a permanent feature on Walton Street before the First World War. To the right are Chapman's Tea Rooms. (T. Green).

Boxing Shows were always good attractions. The show-fronts gave artists the opportunity to paint famous fighters and fights on the canvas banners. This is Harry Hughes' "Assault at Arms" booth. (T. Green).

Looking down another row of rides, with the terraced houses of Walton Street in the background. John Collins' Steam Yachts, then called "Baltic" and "Oceanic" after the White Star Liners, are on the left of the view, behind which are William Murphy's Switchback and a manually-propelled Bicycle roundabout.

When Waddingtons patented Motor Cars for Switchbacks in 1905, many of the old, gilded Gondola cars were replaced by the latest "Racing Motor Cars". Notice how even this early the signs warned: "Beware Police Traps"! (A. Cook).

Motor Cars even replaced horses on other roundabouts. These ladies are riding on Marshall's "Flying Motors", converted from a set of Galloping Horses. The steam centre engine can be seen behind the car.

Marshall's Motors again in this general view of the 1906 Fair. Behind them is a set of Steam Swings and to the left are two Strikers, where lads had the opportunity to show off their strength.

Another general view of the 1906 fair. Lieske's Revolving Cars and William Shipley's Galloping Horses are lost amongst the dense crowds at the corner of the two main avenues of roundabouts. George Aspland's Bioscope Show dominates the showline.

A close up view of Aspland's Bioscope Show. The main bill was a Western; Cowboys and Indians were popular even in 1906. The banners again give an indication of the competition at Hull Fair between the shows. The carved pillars suspending the arc lamps still survive at the Thursford Steam Museum in Norfolk, where George Aspland's Switchback is also preserved.

Another of the big Bioscopes: Relph and Pedley's Show marks the zenith in the travelling cinemas. The massive mechanical organ was built in Paris by Charles Marenghi. The stage area in front would be up to 60 feet in length, allowing quite ambitious entertainment to draw the crowds. (J. Ling).

Local showman Albert Richards presented a new novelty in 1906: the Razzle Dazzle. This not only revolved, but also dipped from side to side. To the right is one of the first Helter Skelter's to visit Hull Fair.

John Collins' 4-abreast Galloping Horses which were brought from Liverpool each year. In full swing are his Steam Yachts, "Emperor" and "Empress" at Hull in 1906.

Another view of John Collins' rides, with his brother, Pat Collins' Venetian Gala Gondolas. It must have been a wet year: notice the sawdust spread around the machines.

Looking down on the row of rides in 1907, showing, from left to right, John Collins' Steam Yachts and Gallopers, Pat Collins' "Looping the Loop" Motor Switchback, William Shipley's Gallopers and Lieske's Revolving Cars.

Bostock and Wombwell's Menagerie attended Hull Fair for many years. Unlike most shows, which featured mechanical organs, the menagerie had a live band playing on a stage under the canvas canopy on the left of the showfront. Other shows at the fair included Flora the Girl with 1000 lives, and Sing Fu the Pigtail Mystery Man. (A. Cook).

Another view showing a line up of roundabouts. The photograph is interesting in that it shows the double row of side stalls at the Anlaby Road end of the fairground, with the living waggons tightly packed in between.

The Fair in 1907 showing one of the most popular rides to attend Hull for many years. The Steam Yachts were new to Waddingtons, but attended regularly as Harry Lee's until the mid-1970s. Behind, Marshall's Flying Motors can be seen in action.

As well as the Bioscope shows along the show line were Chipperfield's Menagerie, and, at the extreme right, Paulo's Circus performing behind the Bioscope Showfront of John Proctor. (A. Cook).

Two views of Hull Fair in this Art Nouveau style Postcard of the 1908 Fair. (Hull College of Further Education).

An action shot of Relph and Pedley's Razzle Dazzle, with the same firm's Motor Car Switchback to the right, at Hull Fair in 1908. The firm sold out of the travelling business during the First World War.

To the left is Enoch Farrar's Bioscope, with the paraders swinging beneath the banner; to the right is Marshall Brothers' big show. Both families still attend Hull Fair. By the time this photograph was taken the showmen were competing not only with one another but also with the permanent cinemas. (T. Green).

Randall Williams exhibited the first moving pictures at Hull Fair in his Ghost Show in 1896. Ever the enterprising showman, he and his sons Randall and James, kept their show up-to-date. In 1910 he was advertising the "latest animated pictures" and "also the most powerful organ in the World". A product of Gavioli et Cie of Paris, it is shown in this posed shot, with family, workmen and dogs. (Hull College of Further Education).

Enoch Farrar owned no less than three Bioscope Shows before the First World War. This was his ultimate show, "The National Academy of Living Pictures", in 1909 with a massive 112 keyless Gavioli organ. It was reputed at the time to be the largest organ to be imported into Britain.

Behind the crowds at the fair in 1909 are the Cake Walks of Albert Richards and Joe Corrigan. Richard's Cake Walk still attends Hull Fair, now owned by Bishtons.

Looking towards Walton street, the ride nearest the camera is Waddington's "Original Patent" Motors, competing alongside Green's Argyle Model Motors, Aspland's Switchback and Marshall's Switchback. The hand-cart in front of Waddington's ride is from a Steam Laundry in Pullman Street.

1910 was notable for the appearance of the first Scenic Railway. Farrar and Tylers claimed, at the time, that theirs was the only machine of its class in existence. It is shown here at Hull that year alongside Holdsworth's "Alpine Glasade" Helter Skelter. Although there are crowds at the fair, the Scenic is empty!

In the centre of Farrar's Scenic Railway was this gorgeous Gavioli organ. It was a 112 keyless instrument brought from Paris specially for the new ride.

Farrar's Scenic Railway can be seen at the end of the avenue of shows next to the Helter Skelter. Competing together on the left are the Motors of Goldthorpe Marshall, which was converted to a Scenic Railway for Hull in 1910, and the steam Switchbacks of George Aspland and George Green. (Michael Smith).

One of the crazes of 1910 was the Joy Wheel. Several attended the fair that year, including George Green's. To the right of the Joy Wheel was another of Green's attractions, the "House that Jack Built", an early type of Fun-House.

The interior of Green's Joy Wheel, showing the highly polished disc on which riders sat until the speed picked up sufficiently to throw them off into the crowd. The craze was only short lived! (T. Green).

The very popular Pigs and Balloons of Messrs. Relph and Pedley. The spinning balloons had the reputation for being ridden only by those with strong stomachs. The top rotated the opposite way to the platforms.

Pre-World War 1 post-card of Hull Fair showing

William Marshall's Switchback	Albert Richards' Cake Walk	Bostock & Wombwell's Menagerie
Proctor's Circus	Greens' Wiggle Waggle	William Marshall's Switchback
General View	Two Strikers	The Showline

Postcard showing scenes from Hull fair in the early 1920s.

Showmen always had to keep up-to-date with rides and shows. George Green had another new attraction in 1912, the Wiggle Woggle. Riders sat on bench seats on a platform mounted on rollers; another set of rollers was set at 90 degrees to the first, giving an exhilarating ride and causing quite a spectacle.

Amongst the shows in 1912 was Christina the Tattooed Princess, direct from Paris, presented by Tom Wortley. Only when she was on the inside of the show would Christina have shown the paying public her unusual features. Perhaps even at this early stage the showmen were concerned by public attitudes as one sign states: "NOT a Peep Show". (J. Ling).

Another action shot showing Turner's Razzle Dazzle in motion, with Gledstone's Wiggle Woggle and Richard's Cake Walk.

An endless throng of people between the showline and the avenues of rides. The Scenic Railway in the foreground belonged to Pat Collins M.P. from Walsall. (T. Green).

In striking contrast to the barrel organs showmen used on their early shows and rides is this Marenghi fair organ. As the placard says: "This orchestra has just arrived direct from Paris", and was indeed new at Hull Fair 1913. It was built for Goldthorpe Marshall and was used in his Scenic Railway. So versatile was the instrument that it was used to give recitals on Sunday evenings in aid of local charities.

A view which gives an impression of the number of small shows which appeared at Hull Fair every year. A couple of rides, a Cake Walk and a Wiggle Woggle, have already taken the place of shows. (T. Green).

Despite the outbreak of war the fair was allowed to go ahead in 1914. The show on the left with painted canvas banners above the entrance is typical of many shows which attended the fair, even before its move to Walton Street. Towards the right of the view is "Convict City" a show which displayed a working model made by a prisoner during his fifteen year sentence. (T. Green).

Most showmen sent their waggons on the railways, but they still had to be collected and brought to Walton Street behind the engines. In this view Harniess' Gallopers are being hauled by their Fowler showman's engine "Dreadnought". The first load is the centre truck, the last two are living wagons. The large engine wheels are running on steel strakes, no wonder the vibrations over the cobble sets caused local residents to complain that they shook their houses.

The last Hull Fair before being interrupted by the First World War. The Tiny Lady on the right is billed as the "World's Wonder" whilst the show to the left goes one better proclaiming that it has been patronised by the "Elite of the Universe"! (T. Green).

THE INTER-WAR YEARS 1919-1939

Back to Walton Street in 1919 after World War 1. Bostock and Wombwell's Menagerie dominates the shot. Billy the Pelican can be seen helping to attract crowds on the right of the stage, On the left is Mander's show, no longer a waxworks, but by now another Menagerie. (Michael Smith).

Scenery inside Harniess Brothers' Scenic Railway included a waterfall cascading above the paybox, illuminated by changing coloured lamps. The authentic reproduction Motor Cars are in the forefront, complete with steering wheels.

Behind the scenes: Jack Whyatt's Steam Yachts, "Victory" and "Renown" with his Foster showman's engine "Queen Mary" in the foreground. The tall chimney helped to take the smoke above the rides and people.

An attraction which has remained popular at Hull Fair since its introduction in 1906 is the Helter Skelter. Harniess Brothers' "Big Dip" was unusual in the severe fall in the chutes half-way down the tower. Riders would have been able to get really good speed up coming down here.

Crowds fill Walton Street fairground in this 1920s view showing Aspland's Gondola Switchback and Pat Ross Collins' Motor Scenic Railway. In the background is Johnson's Cake Walk and a Helter Skelter. (J. Schofield).

Virtually the same view of the fair, but taken further along the line of rides. There is something strange about the shot, however, because although the ground is packed with people, the rides are all closed, with canvas across their fronts. It may have been taken on a Sunday, when concerts were given and speakers attended the fair. (T. Green).

Another busy afternoon. Crowds are seen milling between Tippler White's Chair-o-Planes and Ling's Yachts on the left and Farrar Brothers' two Scenic Railways on the right.

After the First World War, Lieske's Wheel, with only four of its original eight cars remaining, was to make only a few more appearances. The Chair-o-Planes were a new attraction in the early 1920s. They were electrically-driven and most were imported from Germany. The structure to the left is a Jack and Jill Slide.

Looking towards Walton Street in 1922. The first ride on the right is Pat Collins' Whale Island Scenic Railway, with its front supported by magnificent carved and gilded Atlante figures. Beyond are Aspland's Switchback, Marshall's Scenic Railway and Holdsworth's Pigs and Balloons.

By the late 1920s new novelty rides were beginning to appear. The first ride on the avenue, to the left of the shot, is William Marshall's Hey Day. The ride next in line is Corrigan's Galloping Horses. Beyond these are Holdsworth's Pigs and Balloons and Goldthorpe Marshall's Scenic Railway. In the distance can be seen one of the first Walls of Death to visit Hull. (T. Green).

In 1933 Reuben Holdsworth's Pigs and Balloons made their final visit to Hull. Here workmen are seen cleaning the brass handrails ready for opening.

Joe Ling's Steam Yachts, "Shamrock" and "Valerie" attended Hull Fair from being new in 1921. A contemporary style of living waggon can be seen to the right of the shot. (J. Ling).

Brand new to Hull Fair in 1931 was Joe Ling's Ghost Train. It was built by Orton, Sons and Spooner of Burton on Trent. The idea of the dark ride is a very popular one, and new Ghost Trains are still being built. (J. Ling).

Hull Fair 1935 with one of the earliest Walls of Death to attend Hull Fair. The main attraction on Barry's Sensational Motordrome was the American Lion Tamer, the Fearless Egbert, who carried Monarch the Lion in his sidecar. Notice how the legend of Bostocks lived on after 1931 with the zoo on the right. (Michael Smith).

Another shot of the 1935 fair. In addition to the roundabouts, Hull Fair has hundreds of feet of side stalls. To the left are the throwing games, mainly coconut sheets. The boxes of wooden balls can be seen at the front of each stall. At the bottom of the avenue on the showline is a Wall of Death. (Hull College of Further Education).

The junction of Anlaby Road and Walton Street during the Fair. A policeman on point duty stands between the two public houses, and the end of the stalls, which stretch the whole length of the street, can be seen behind him. (C. Ketchell).

Preparations were well advanced for the 1932 Hull Fair when this shot was taken. On the left is Marshall's Chair-o-Planes next to which is Shaw's Dodgem Track. The truck on the right is stacked with cans of petrol. (C. Ketchell).

Another shot which shows how tightly packed the fairground is. The terraces along Walton Street are visible, with Wrigglesworth's Memorial Works. In the forefront are side stalls and living waggons. The Gallopers are Morley's and Marshall's Hey Day is the other ride seen on the left. (C. Ketchell).

The entrance to the fairground from Walton Street. On the left is Green's Caterpillar, whilst right at the bottom of the ground is the Palm Beach Company's Figure-8 Railway and Pat Collins' Water Dodgems at Hull in 1932. (C. Ketchell).

The atmosphere is strangely missing when the crowds are taken away. This view was taken in 1932 looking towards the houses at the Spring Bank end of Walton Street fairground. On the left is Farrar's Noah's Ark, Mander's Steam Yachts, Jack Whyatt's Steam Yachts and Swirl. Across the avenue is Pat Collins' Ghost Train, Farrar's Mont Blanc and Ling's Steam Yachts. (C. Ketchell).

A Postcard from Hull Fair in 1936. The top views show Barry's Wall of Death and Corrigan's Speedway; at the bottom are Chicken Joe's grocery stall and Ling's Ghost Train. (J. Ling).

Another view of Hull Fair in 1932, showing the same roundabouts, but looking from above Farrar's Dodgem Track. The engines can be seen behind the rides. They had to be close as they generated power for driving the rides and the electric lights. (C. Ketchell).

Aerial shot of Hull Fair taken by Malcolm Slater of York. Note the changes in the buildings surrounding the fair, but how similar the layout of the rides and attractions is to the 1950s. Photo courtesy of Aerofilms Ltd.

One of the last side shows to attend Hull Fair is Wheatley's George the Gentle Giant. George Gracie, born at Forth in 1938, stands 7'3" tall. This view of the show was taken in 1977. (M. Smith).

Children's corner near to the Drill Hall has featured several favourites over the years. Many will remember Crow's Double Deck Juvenile ride. Austin Cars, Fire Engines and other toys were on the bottom deck, whilst above was a row of rockets. The idea was patented by Crows in the 1950s.

In 1988 Pat Collins brought the Thunderbird, a European ride with a mass of lighting both on the ride and on the "flash" across the back. In these cases the showman's engines have given way to three-phase 440v generators.

"Bigger, Brighter & Better than Ever" is the claim made by Joe Barak, alias Chicken Joe, "The Man you all Know". Of all the dozens of stalls at Hull, it is peculiar that one stall should be so well remembered by so many people. (Hull College of Further Education).

Another view of Chicken Joe's stall at Hull in 1935. The showman's engine with its extension chimney in place can be seen on the left. (Hull College of Further Education).

The early Noah's Ark rides were from Germany, but once Robert Lakin of Streatham began to develop the concept, they became much more elaborate. Ling's ride was known as the Ben Hur as the big front featured a Roman Chariot Racing scene. Rather incongruously the rounding boards featured jungle scenery and the bottom shutters were Venetian canal scenes.

POST WAR 1945-1990

Tippler White and his sons, Clifford and Johnny, have brought many shows to Hull Fair over the years. The attraction for 1947 was "The World's Heaviest Married Couple". Barny and Joy, the Australian Giant and Giantess were making their first visit to Hull that year.

Many themes for fairground rides have been inspired by films. In the 1930s it was Ben Hur; in the 1980s Ghostbusters lent itself for the decoration of this Matterhorn owned by Michael Wallis. It is seen here at Hull Fair in 1988.

The last steam-driven ride at Hull Fair. Harry Lee's Steam Yachts, presented by Fred Coupland at Hull in 1988. The ride, new in 1901 and built in King's Lynn by Savages, attended Hull Fair regularly from new, in the ownership of Waddingtons. It is still powered by a Savage steam engine, and music is provided by a 46-key Chiappa fair-organ.

Painted by Orton, Sons and Spooner in the mid-1930s, this scene forms the front for a ride which attended Hull Fair until the late-1980s. Although faded under browning varnish, this period-piece was photographed at Hull in 1980.

Originally built for Aspland's Bioscope Show, this mammoth organ was built in Paris by Gavioli et Cie, described in their catalogue as "Concert Militaire et Concert Symphonique". It was rebuilt in 1928 and placed in the centre of the Gondola Switchback. It can be seen in the photograph of Aspland's Show taken before World War One.

Side shows have largely disappeared since the war. Bert Hughes' Boxing Pavilion, seen here in 1947, was the last to visit Hull Fair. Boxing as an organised sport has changed enormously and boxers no longer begin their career in fairground booths as they might have in the past.

Since the days of the Ghost Show, the concept of the Haunted House has existed on the fairground. Now just a darkened Fun-House which appeals to youngsters with a macabre fear of the dark, and possibly to slightly older couples who find the darkness attractive for other reasons. Willie Marshall's Haunted House is seen at Hull in 1947.

The final visit of a Scenic Railway to Hull Fair. By 1948 Pat Collins' Dragons and Peacocks ride had lost much of its grace; the front boards had originally depicted a classical Greek scene, but this had been redecorated with St. George slaying the Dragon. The canopy of the showman's engine, "The Griffin", which brought the ride can just be seen to the left alongside Hoadley's Scammell tractor.

On a visit from the North-East in 1948 was John Hoadley's Moonrocket. The uniformed attendants are in white overalls. Inside, a figure of the famous cartoon character, Popeye, used to ride a smaller rocket in the centre, the opposite way to the riders, creating the illusion they were moving even faster.

This Atlante figure is one of the carved figures on the organ, originally part of the Bioscope Showfront. Others, including dancing ladies and cherubs, also survive in different collections.

The new novelty rides of the 1980s all tried to go one better than the competition. Many of the new rides are continental, like this Traum Boot or Dream Boat, presented at the 1987 fair by Pat Collins.

Twilight at Hull in 1988. Lighting is a very important part of the attraction of the fair. Dominating the skyline is John Ayers' Skyline Helter Skelter.

The Skydiver is an American ride travelled by Eastern Counties showman, William Summers. This 1988 shot gives some impression of the scale of the machine.

Wheatley's "Shooting the Rapids", seen here in 1948, standing alongside Marshall's Wall of Death. The last Wall of Death to attend Hull Fair was in the 1970s when Messhams brought their show through from the Goose Fair. Wheatley's still bring their novelty, now called the "Outer Limits".

Joe Shaw's Speedway at Hull Fair in 1948. Remarkably when this ride last appeared at Hull in 1987 it had hardly changed. The front boards still carried their original paintwork showing 1930s racing cars, motorcycles and bi-plane, as painted by Orton, Sons and Spooner. The Cake Walk to the left still attends the fair.

Terry Atha issues orders to his staff during the build up of his "Hell Blazer" Waltzer. Notice how accurately the rides have to be positioned: if just one was a matter of inches out the whole ground layout could be affected. (Bernard Mitchell).

The view down Walton Street before the fair opened. This 1949 shot shows some of the stalls outside West Park. The old bus is typical of hundreds of such vehicles which were used by showmen for canteens, packing trucks and even living vans after their days carrying passengers. This old Leyland bus, used by McBaines, had been driven down from Kirkcaldy for the fair.

A view further down Walton Street the same year. Amongst the stalls and canteens are numerous palmists and fortune tellers, another tradition which has outlived the various changes through which the fair has gone.

Looking over the fair towards the carriage sheds and Hymers College. The show line along the back still features a Wall of Death and Fossett's Circus. The rides seen from the back are Joe Ling's Ben Hur and Shaw's Dodgems and Moonrocket. In the foreground amid side stalls, hooplas and packing trucks is a Helter Skelter. (Hull College of Further Education).

Harry Lee's Yachts have been a favourite at Hull Fair for many years. They are often called Shamrocks by locals, as the boats have been named "Shamrock" and "Columbia" since new. The names came originally from racing yachts. This view of the Yachts was taken in 1950. They ceased to travel when their owner retired, but made a return in 1989 to be the last steam-driven ride to attend the fair.

Bob Carver's Fish and Chip bar from Hull Market which opens at the Drill Hall entrance to the fairground each year. This view was taken in 1953.

A remarkable shot of the 1952 Hull Fair, taken by Aerofilms. This gives an idea of the scale of the fair, and how so much equipment packs on to the fourteen acre site. The layout of the fair can be traced back many years, and has changed very little since. Walton Street can be seen packed with stalls, and no less than 38 roundabouts can be identified. Add to these hundreds of feet of side stalls, dozens of hooplas and a full size circus, as well as all the transport needed to bring it all. To make it all fit is a mammoth task. The street has altered perhaps as much as the fair. The new Walton Street Club was built some years ago and the terraces have been demolished. (Courtesy of Aerofilms Ltd.).

Another local firm who used to sell their produce on the fairground were Padgetts. One of their Ice Cream parlours is seen here in 1953.

Syncopating Sandy is seen playing non-stop on Shufflebottom's Show. Usually a Wild West show, for 1953 it featured the pianist who managed to play for 156 hours non-stop. The show to the right offered the illusion of a vanishing motor-cycle!

The opening ceremony in 1953 took place from the stage on Tom Norman's Palladium Show. This was the last show at Hull with a fair-organ on the front. The attraction that year was Ian Fraser's team of World war II divers re-enacting a wartime operation.
(Hull Leisure Services).

Hull was one of the last big fairs to offer a circus and menagerie amongst its attractions. Bailey's Menagerie and Sir Robert Fossett's Circus are shown at Hull in 1955.

Walter Ling's Waltzer at Hull in 1956, capturing the art deco style of the Odeon Cinema. Farrars, Lings and Collins all featured this idea, but the big front boards proved a great deal of work to build up and were often quickly discarded.

Even by the mid-1950s when this view was taken, Galloping Horses were an old time ride. Billy Manning brought this set to Hull Fair in 1955. Although they were originally steam, modernisation had taken place, and they were electrically driven when they visited Hull. The ride still survives at an amusement park on Clarence Pier at Southsea.

A walk down Walton Street at night past the endless stalls offering Brandy Snap, Nougat and Candy Floss. (Bernard Mitchell).

While many aspects of Hull Fair have changed enormously, compare this night shot of Bob Carver's Fish and Chip bar taken in the late 1980s, with the 1953 shot. (Bernard Mitchell).

As soon as the fair shuts on Saturday night, the showmen begin the task of dismantling all the equipment. By day-break all that can be seen of most of the rides is a lorry and trailer. The previous night Theodore Whyatt's Skid had been open, by the early hours of Sunday morning it is neatly packed onto his Foden lorry and centre truck. (Bernard Mitchell).

"The Monster's Revenge"! J. C. Crow & Sons' ride ready for its journey back to the north-east. The Atkinson tractor, which began life with Pickford's Haulage, is ready with the generators and part of the ride. The ghostly image of the "Traum Boat" looms in the background ready to be dismantled. (Bernard Mitchell).

The morning after: a week's rubbish cleared away and the site is clear again giving few clues as to the past week's activities. Anyone who has seen the fairground can only wonder how everything is made to fit. (Bernard Mitchell).